BABOUSHKA

Adapted from a Russian folktale

Retold by Helen Bethune
Illustrated by Elise Hurst

Longman

Sydney, Melbourne, Brisbane, Perth and
associated companies around the world

A long time ago, in a land far away, snow
swirled around a tiny hut. In that hut lived
Baboushka.

Inside her hut, Baboushka stacked wood into her stove to keep her home warm and snug. The old woman's hut was small and bare. She worked hard to keep it clean and tidy.

Baboushka's cat dozed by the glow of the fire as she swept and scrubbed, dusted and cleaned, each night.

One winter's evening, Baboushka heard the
sound of trumpets over the howls of the wind.

She looked out of her window and saw a long procession approaching her hut.

First, came a wonderful sleigh lit by a lantern. It was drawn by four magnificent white horses.

In the sleigh, there were three noblemen. They wore splendid hats and shimmering jewels. They were dressed in fine, fur-lined cloaks.

Guards on horses rode behind the sleigh. Then
came men on foot, carrying lanterns. They
trudged through the deep snow.

The procession halted outside Baboushka's hut.
The tallest of the noblemen rapped on the door
with his staff. The old woman hesitantly opened
the door and peered out.

At first, Baboushka was almost blinded by the snow and the force of the wind. But then, through the whirling snow, she saw the three stately noblemen.

The tallest nobleman said, 'We are looking for a newborn baby, but we have become lost in the snowstorm. We must find this child. We bring gifts for him. Can you help us, Baboushka? You know your way in this place.'

Baboushka stared at him in wonder. She looked at the snow whipping around outside. She looked back at her cosy hearth, where Anastasia, her cat, was curled up by the stove.

Baboushka turned back to the noblemen and said, 'Good sirs, this is a fearsome storm. It is perilous to continue your search tonight. Come, stay with me, and we will set out in the morning to look for the child.'

The nobleman replied, 'There is no time, Baboushka. We must make haste. We must leave now.'

With that, the noblemen turned from her, and the entire procession set off, back into the raging storm.

Her day's work finally finished, Baboushka sat and ate her supper. Her hut was warm and cosy, but she felt strangely sad.

She could not stop thinking about the newborn baby the noblemen were looking for. She wondered what the child meant to them.

'He must be very important,' Baboushka said to Anastasia. 'Maybe I should go and look for him too, or at least help the noblemen find their way through the storm.'

At first light, Baboushka set off to follow the noblemen. She trudged through the snow, wrapped in her thick shawl.

She took gifts for the baby.

They were humble gifts, but precious because they were all she had.

The falling snow had covered all traces of the noblemen's journey. It was impossible to know which way the procession had gone.

But Baboushka was determined to find them.

She asked everyone she met whether they had seen the procession. No one had seen it go by.

She rapped on doors in the villages she passed through, asking after the noblemen.

No one had seen them.

Baboushka gave a small gift with each person she spoke.

She left a little happiness behind her.

Baboushka never found the noblemen. She travelled a long way but she never discovered where they went.

However, everywhere she had been, people felt someone good had passed their way.

In that faraway land, people believe that
Baboushka still searches each winter, looking
for the noblemen and the newborn baby.

Each year at that time, children wait for
Baboushka. They never see her, but in the
morning they find the gifts she has left behind
sitting on their doorsteps.